Enjoy!

SHORT WALKS
WINCHESTER

by Malcolm Leatherdale

Malcolm Leatherdale

Fishing on the River Test at Wherwell (Walk 14)

CONTENTS

USING THIS GUIDE

Routes in this book

In this book you will find a selection of easy or moderate walks suitable for almost everyone, including casual walkers and families with children, or for when you only have a short time to fill. The routes have been carefully chosen to allow you to explore the area and its attractions. Although there may be some climbs there is no challenging terrain, but do bear in mind that conditions can sometimes be wet or muddy underfoot. A route summary table is included on page 6 to help you choose the right walk.

Clothing and footwear

You won't need any special equipment to enjoy these walks. The weather in Britain can be changeable, so choose clothing suitable for the season and wear or carry a waterproof jacket. For footwear, comfortable walking boots or trainers with a good grip are best. A small rucksack for drinks, snacks and spare clothing is useful. See www.adventuresmart.uk.

Walk descriptions

At the beginning of each walk you'll find all the information you need:

- start/finish location, with postcode and a what3words address to help you find it
- parking and transport information, estimated walking time, total distance and climb
- details of public toilets available along the route and where you can get refreshments
- a summary of the key highlights of the walk and what you might see

Timings given are the time to complete the walk at a reasonable walking pace. Allow extra time for extended stops or if walking with children.

The route is described in clear, easy-to-follow directions, with each waypoint marked on an accompanying map extract. It's a good idea to read the whole of the route instructions before setting out, so that you know what to expect.

Maps, GPX files and what3words

Extracts from the OS® 1:25,000 map accompany each route. GPX files for all the walks in this book are available to download at www.cicerone.co.uk/1164/gpx.

What3words is a free smartphone app which identifies every 3m square of the globe with a unique three-word address, e.g. ///destiny.cafe.sonic. For more information see https://what3words.com/products/what3words-app.

Walking with children

Even young children can be surprisingly strong walkers, but every family is different and you may need to adapt the timings given in this book to take that into account. Make sure you go at the pace of the slowest member and choose a walk with an exciting objective in mind, such as a cave, river, waterfall or picnic spot. Many of the walks can be shortened to suit – suggestions are included at the end of the route description.

Dogs

Sheep or cattle may be found grazing on a number of these walks. Keep dogs under control at all times so that they don't scare or disturb livestock or wildlife. Cattle, particularly cows with calves, may very occasionally pose a risk to walkers with dogs. If you ever feel threatened by cattle, you should let go of your dog's lead and let it run free.

Enjoying the countryside responsibly

Enjoy the countryside and treat it with respect to protect our natural environments. Stick to footpaths and take your litter home with you. When driving, slow down on rural roads and park considerately, or better still use public transport. For more details check out www.gov.uk/countryside-code.

The Countryside Code

Respect everyone
- be considerate to those living in, working in and enjoying the countryside
- leave gates and property as you find them
- do not block access to gateways or driveways when parking
- be nice, say hello, share the space
- follow local signs and keep to marked paths unless wider access is available

Protect the environment
- take your litter home – leave no trace of your visit
- do not light fires and only have BBQs where signs say you can
- always keep dogs under control and in sight
- dog poo – bag it and bin it – any public waste bin will do
- care for nature – do not cause damage or disturbance

Enjoy the outdoors
- check your route and local conditions
- plan your adventure – know what to expect and what you can do
- enjoy your visit, have fun, make a memory

ROUTE SUMMARY TABLE

WALK NAME	START POINT	TIME	DISTANCE
1. Winchester Cathedral, St Cross and Tun Bridge	The Broadway, Winchester	1¾hr	7km (4¼ miles)
2. St Catherine's Hill, Hockley Viaduct and Kingsgate	The Broadway, Winchester	2hr	7.5km (4¾ miles)
3. Hyde Gate, Kings Worthy, Abbots Worthy and Easton	Hyde Gate, Winchester	2¾hr	10.5km (6½ miles)
4. Chilcomb and the South Downs Way	The Broadway, Winchester	2hr	8km (5 miles)
5. City Mill, St Giles Hill and Wolvesey Castle	The Broadway, Winchester	1hr	3km (1¾ miles)
6. Westgate, St Cross and Shawford	Westgate, Winchester	1¾hr	6.5km (4 miles)
7. Cheriton, Hinton Ampner and Kilmeston	School Road, Cheriton	2hr	7.5km (4¾ miles)
8. New Alresford, Abbotstone and Old Alresford	Broad Street, New Alresford	2½hr	9km (5½ miles)
9. Itchen Stoke and Ovington	Itchen Stoke village green	1¾hr	6.5km (4 miles)
10. Itchen Abbas, Martyr Worthy, Easton and Avington	Itchen Abbas church	1¾hr	7km (4¼ miles)
11. Stockbridge Down	Eastern end of Stockbridge Down	1hr	3.5km (2¼ miles)
12. Stockbridge and Houghton	High Street, Stockbridge	2¼hr	9.5km (6 miles)
13. Micheldever, Stoke Charity, Hunton and Wonston	Duke Street, Micheldever	2¾hr	10.5km (6½ miles)
14. Wherwell and Chilbolton Cow Common	Wherwell sports field	1¼hr	5km (3 miles)
15. Longparish	Longparish village hall	1½hr	6km (3¾ miles)

HIGHLIGHTS

Cathedral, medieval almshouse and palace ruins

Palace ruins, hill fort and Victorian viaduct

History, nature and a pretty village

South Downs, views and scenic village

Panoramic view of Winchester

Fortified medieval gateway, Cathedral and almshouse

Battle site, country house and South Downs

Handsome Georgian town and the River Alre

Chalk downland and the River Itchen

River Itchen, meadows and thatched villages

Rare chalk downland with great views

Test Way, historic Georgian town and the River Test

Pretty thatched villages

Thatched village, nature reserve and the River Test

Thatched village, meadows and the River Test

SYMBOLS USED ON ROUTE MAPS

(S) Start point

(F) Finish point

(SF) Start and finish at the same place

4→ Waypoint

〜 Route line

MAPPING IS SHOWN AT A SCALE OF 1:25,000

0 KM 0.25 0.5

0 miles 0.25

DOWNLOAD THE GPX FILES FOR FREE AT
www.cicerone.co.uk/1164/GPX

Winchester High Street and the overhanging clock (Walk 6)

INTRODUCTION

River Test at Longparish (Walk 15)

The middle of Hampshire is a vibrant land with sloping tree-clad hills and sweeping chalk downland – all set against the backdrop of a fascinating history and unique geology. When you add the vast array of wildflowers, plants and wildlife that inhabit the various Sites of Special Scientific Interest (SSSI) – in particular Stockbridge Down (see Walk 11) and Chilbolton Cow Common (see Walk 14) – it is not difficult to understand the attraction of a place that so completely defines pastoral England.

Nor can we forget the sparkling chalk streams that have famously been described as 'gin clear'. There are only about 200 of these rarest of streams worldwide and 160 of those are in England, with the finest in Hampshire, including the internationally renowned Rivers Itchen, Meon and Test.

And in the midst of this glorious setting stands historic Winchester.

The city was a strategic settlement for the Romans, who arrived in around AD70. It was only 12 miles from the port of Clausentum on the eastern side of today's Southampton and at a time when the River Itchen was quite navigable. Winchester became the fifth largest Roman city in England.

The accessibility of Winchester also made it a focal point for trade. Fairs that attracted merchants from a wide area including Europe were held on the top of St Giles Hill (see Walk 5). The Roman name for Winchester was Venta Belgarum, which loosely means 'the market place of the Belgae', and is attributable to a Celtic tribe who arrived to colonise St Catherine's Hill in about 100BC (see Walks 1 and 2).

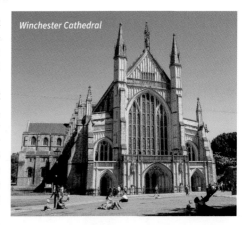

Winchester Cathedral

Winchester was at the very heart of Wessex, the Anglo-Saxon kingdom, and played a pivotal role in England's medieval history as the nation's capital before London eventually assumed the role.

Alfred the Great's connection with Winchester began in AD871 when he was crowned king of Wessex after the death (probably as a result of wounds incurred in a battle with the Vikings) of his older brother Aethelred. The commanding statue of Alfred in the city centre was erected in 1901 to commemorate the millennial anniversary of his death in AD899. The statue, standing close to the former Roman Eastgate, is cast in bronze with a plinth of Cornish granite.

Hovering in the background is the 9th-century bishop St Swithun, very much part of the folklore of Winchester and patron saint of the Cathedral. The relics or remains of St Swithun, who had died in AD863, were exhumed from outside the rebuilt Old Minster (the original 7th-century cathedral church of Wessex) to be transferred inside just as the heavens opened on 15 July 971.

Tradition now decrees that if it rains on 15 July, St Swithun's feast day, it will continue to rain for 40 days!

Walking in Winchester and the surrounding area

This guidebook contains six walks exploring the city and its historic sites and there are also nine walks in the surrounding areas of the Itchen Valley and Test Valley. Five of the walks (Walks 1–5) start and finish in Winchester and one linear walk (Walk 6) starts in the city but finishes at Shawford, where there is a bus or train option for the return. All the other walks are either circular or out-and-back routes. Some of the walks outside the city (Walks 7–10) can be reached by a regular bus service, but the bus service for Walk 12 is less frequent. The remaining four

Thatched cottages in Wherwell (Walk 14)

walks outside Winchester require a car or short taxi ride.

The walks outside the city all explore the chalk landscape and delightful villages, with most routes alive to the 'sound' of a chalk stream. You will discover many charming villages brimming with flint and thatch with their individual 'hostelries' to match! Two of the walks start and finish in the Georgian towns of New Alresford and Stockbridge so there is something for everyone.

Places to stay

There is a wide range of accommodation in Winchester. The nearby market towns of New Alresford and Stockbridge are also convenient places to stay and where several of the walks in this guidebook are located.

Travel to and from Winchester

Winchester is very well connected to many parts of the UK by road, including the M3 motorway direct from London. The A34 provides connectivity to and from the midlands and the north. The city has a mainline rail station with trains to London Waterloo for links with the midlands and the north.

Winchester itself is quite compact and frequent buses serve all parts of the city. The main place to catch a bus is the Broadway, conveniently alongside King Alfred's statue in the city centre. For those coming into the city by car, Winchester is also ringed by several Park and Ride sites.

King Alfred's statue in the Broadway

WALK 1

Winchester Cathedral, St Cross and Tun Bridge

Time: 1¾hr
Distance: 7km (4¼ miles)
Climb: 20m

An enjoyable stroll exploring Winchester and its pivotal place in the history of England

Start/finish	*King Alfred's statue in the Broadway*
Locate	*SO23 9BE ///paraded.margin.bulge*
Cafes/pubs	*Lots of pubs and cafes in Winchester*
Transport	*Train to Winchester*
Parking	*Park and Ride outside the city and plenty of parking in the centre*
Toilets	*In Abbey Gardens by the Broadway*

This circular walk encapsulates the history of Winchester, including King Alfred's statue, the Cathedral, the Church of St Swithun, the Clarendon Way, the 12th-century Hospital of St Cross, St Catherine's Hill, the 18th-century Itchen Navigation, Tun Bridge and the ruins of Wolvesey Castle.

Keats' Walk

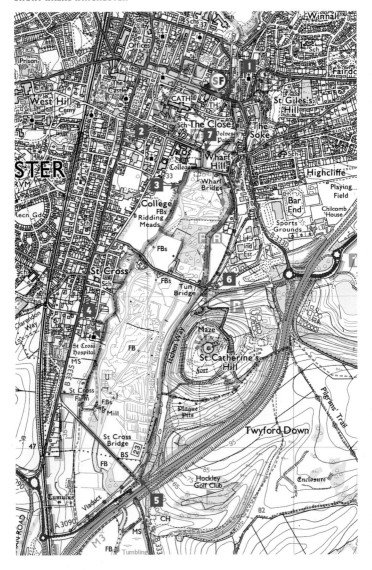

1 Under Alfred's steadfast gaze continue past the Guildhall for about 300m to Market Street and turn left to the majestic Cathedral. Consecrated in 1093, Winchester is the longest medieval cathedral in Europe. Go past the front of the Cathedral and turn left through a stone archway into The Close. At the end of The Close the 15th-century Priors Gate leads through to the 14th-century Kingsgate with the 'miniature' Church of St Swithun-upon-Kingsgate above.

2 Leave under the Kingsgate and turn left into College Street. On your right you pass the house where the novelist Jane Austen spent the last months of her life in 1817. At the end of College Street bear right at the road barrier into College Walk, keeping alongside the brick wall for about 100m to reach a junction. Turn right along the college access road to where it ends by a fingerpost with a Clarendon Way waymark disc pointing you left. You are now following in the footsteps of Romantic poet John Keats.

3 The chalk stream the **River Itchen** appears fleetingly to your left before it edges away. Continue for the remaining 550m to Garnier Road. If you want to shorten your walk turn left along Garnier Road to connect with the

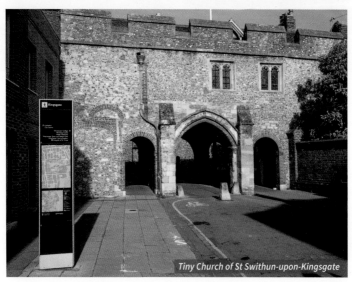

Tiny Church of St Swithun-upon-Kingsgate

St Cross Almshouse

Pilgrims Trail at Waypoint 6. Otherwise cross the road to another Clarendon Way fingerpost slightly to the right and continue for about 500m to the **Hospital of St Cross** and Almshouse of Noble Poverty.

> Founded in 1132, St Cross is home to 25 elderly residents and is said to be England's oldest and 'most perfect' almshouse. The grounds and buildings are open to the public at certain times of the year.

4 Where the Clarendon Way diverts to the right at St Cross, you instead keep straight ahead along the path to a metal kissing gate at the beginning of a short avenue of trees followed by another kissing gate at the end, a third further on and finally a single gate that in a few metres leads to a narrow tarmac closed road, Five Bridges Road. Turn left, cross the River Itchen and continue to the road end.

5 At the end of the road go through the gate to a junction of tarmac paths where the **Itchen Way** now joins. Turn right to lengthen the walk to the former railway viaduct at Hockley. Otherwise follow the broad tarmac path to the left along the Itchen Way, signposted Itchen Navigation Winchester, for about 600m to reach the pedestrian access to **St Catherine's Hill**, the site of an Iron Age hill fort. Close by is the remnant of St Catherine's Lock, once part of the Itchen Navigation (see Walk 2). Continue for another 800m to reach the Garnier Road car park by **Tun Bridge**. Cross the road to join the path signposted Pilgrims Trail.

6 Now follow the Pilgrims Trail alongside the Itchen Navigation and past the college sports field to a footpath. After passing several houses the path veers to the right, hedge-lined and slightly uphill to reach a narrow road. Turn left for about 100m to College Walk and left again to continue along College Walk to the road barrier at the end of College Street where you were earlier.

> (i) *In medieval times the channel of the River Itchen alongside The Weirs, originally created by the Romans as a defensive moat, was almost twice the width it is today.*

7 Turn sharp right at the barrier and go past the entrance to **Wolvesey Castle**, also known as the Old Bishop's Palace (see Walk 5), and keep to the broad tarmac path for about 500m to the road bridge across the river. There is a ramp and a short flight of steps up to the High Street. Turn left to finish at King Alfred's statue.

− To shorten

Between Waypoints 3 and 4, when you reach Garnier Road turn left for about 450m along the pavement to join the Pilgrims Trail on the other side of Tun Bridge at Waypoint 6, saving about 2.5km and 40min.

+ To lengthen

To visit the Hockley railway viaduct, at Waypoint 5 turn sharp right at the junction of paths, signposted for the Viaduct Way (National Cycle Route 23). This adds about 500m each way and 20min to the walk.

Bishop's residence

WALK 2

St Catherine's Hill, Hockley Viaduct and Kingsgate

Start/finish	*King Alfred's statue in the Broadway*
Locate	*SO23 9BE ///paraded.margin.bulge*
Cafes/pubs	*Lots of pubs and cafes in Winchester*
Transport	*Train to Winchester*
Parking	*Park and Ride outside the city and plenty of parking in the centre*
Toilets	*In Abbey Gardens by the Broadway*

Wolvesey Castle, the Itchen Navigation, St Catherine's Hill Iron Age hill fort, the former railway viaduct at Hockley and historic Kingsgate all feature in this fascinating circular walk from Winchester city centre. It spans more than 2000 years of history ranging from a time before the Romans arrived, through the turbulent Anglo-Saxon and Norman periods, and culminating in the illustrious Victorian era.

Time: 2hr
Distance: 7.5km (4¾ miles)
Climb: 10m

This easy amble includes the ruins of medieval Wolvesey Castle, an Iron Age hill fort and unique Victorian industrial heritage

Hockley Viaduct

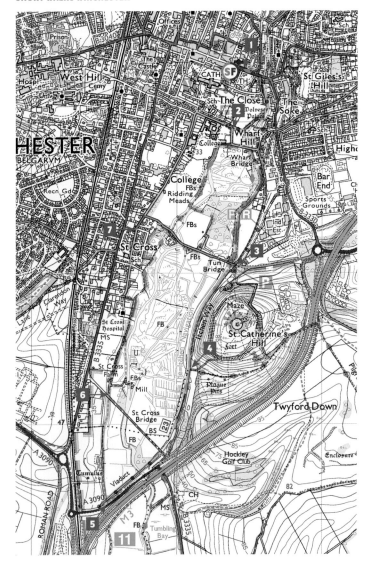

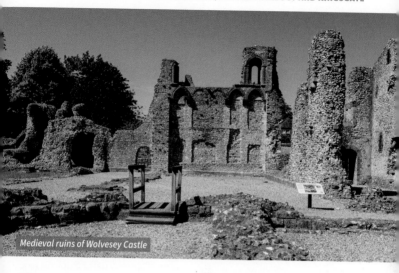

Medieval ruins of Wolvesey Castle

1 From the back of King Alfred's statue walk about 100m towards the road bridge over the cascading River Itchen. At the bridge follow the sign on the right for South Downs Way and Viaduct Way and descend the ramp and short flight of steps to the broad tarmac path called The Weirs. Keep to the path for about 500m as it draws alongside the medieval flint wall edging around to the right and marking the boundary with the remnants of **Wolvesey Castle** (see Walk 5). As you reach the entrance to Wolvesey, next to the present-day bishop's residence, bear left along College Walk.

2 In about another 100m at the junction with a college access road turn left for about 200m, still heading along College Walk, to reach the residential road Wharf Hill. Here follow the sign for the Viaduct Way to the right, which brings you into a narrow road and the Itchen Way. After about 30m ignore a gate on your right waymarked as the Itchen Way and instead continue for another 70m to a footpath fingerpost on your right pointing you to a hedge-lined path going slightly downhill. Continue alongside the **Itchen Navigation** and past a college sports field to Garnier Road where you cross to the car park by **Tun Bridge** and re-join National Cycle Route 23 at the end of the car park.

St Catherine's Hill

3 Keep to the broad tarmac path, with the Itchen Navigation on your right, for about 800m to **St Catherine's Hill**.

St Catherine's Hill is an Iron Age hill fort that dominates the chalk downland hereabouts. It is now a nature reserve and Site of Special Scientific Interest. Near the entrance is the remnant of St Catherine's Lock, once part of the Itchen Navigation.

4 Continue along the path for 600m to the former **railway viaduct** at Hockley, then walk across the viaduct itself. Built in 1891, Hockley Viaduct is an impressive piece of engineering, 600m long and 12m high, with 33 arches. The line was closed in the early 1960s.

5 At the end of the viaduct, leave the NCR23 and bear left to walk along the footpath on the wide grass verge by the side of the road slightly downhill for about 150m. A few metres short of a layby join a narrow tarmac footpath, turning sharp left through woodland to reach a metal kissing gate at the base of the viaduct. Bear right to a fingerpost directing you through a meadow. This leads in about 300m to another metal kissing gate way-marked the Valley of Fields and fronting a path that edges left over a brick culvert. Continue through a nar-row field to a broader meadow and head to the far right-hand corner and another metal kissing gate out onto the closed Five Bridges Road.

6 Cross the road to a stony access track. After about 50m a single gate bearing a St Cross Almshouse information board is immediately followed by another metal kissing gate at the side of a stream. Continue through the meadow to a short avenue of trees with St Cross on your left (see Walk 1). At the end of the avenue a metal kissing gate opens out to a wide path skirting the front of **St Cross Hospital**. By the corner go left for about 50m along the Clarendon Way to the entrance to St Cross. Then immediately turn right by a white road barrier into St Cross Back Street, which leads to St Faiths Road. Stay straight ahead at the next junction into Kingsgate Road.

7 Continue for about 900m along Kingsgate Road then Kingsgate Street until you reach the Church of St Swithun-upon-Kingsgate close by the historic Wykeham Arms. Turn right along College Street to the road barrier at the end where you bear left past Wolvesey Castle and retrace your outward route to King Alfred's statue.

━ To shorten

Walk as far as St Catherine's Hill and back, saving about 2.5km and 40min.

✚ To lengthen

For a grandstand view of Winchester climb the 'stairway' to the top of St Catherine's Hill, adding about 250m each way and 15min to the walk.

The Itchen Navigation

The Itchen Navigation began to operate from around 1710 between Winchester and Southampton. Although it is often referred to as a canal, some sections or channels of the Itchen were simply improved or widened and others were just bypassed, hence the description 'Navigation'. It was not commercially very successful, being restricted to carrying items such as coal, iron, stone and timber, and ceased to operate in 1869. One of the principal reasons for its demise was the arrival of the London to Southampton Railway in the 1840s.

Kings Worthy

WALK 3

Hyde Gate, Kings Worthy, Abbots Worthy and Easton

Time: 2¾hr
Distance: 10.5km
(6½ miles)
Climb: 30m

A delightful mixture of medieval history at Hyde Abbey, wildflower-rich Winnall Moors and the rustic charms of the village of Easton

Start/finish	Hyde Gate, Winchester
Locate	SO23 7EJ ///geology.sloping.sparkles
Cafes/pubs	Pubs and cafes in Winchester, pubs in Kings Worthy and Easton
Transport	Train to Winchester (650m from start)
Parking	Park and Ride outside the city and plenty of parking in the centre
Toilets	No public toilets on route

This out-and-back route follows the St Swithun's Way, initially to Kings Worthy and then on to Abbots Worthy. From there you join the Itchen Way, crossing several river channels, before continuing through light woodland and meadow to the charming village of Easton within the South Downs National Park. Return to Winchester by the same route.

Hyde Gate

Hyde Gate is part of the site once occupied by the former monastery Hyde Abbey. Hyde Abbey is where the remains of King Alfred (AD849-899) were transferred around 1110. Comprehensive information boards at the site record the events of the time.

1 With your back to Hyde Gate turn right slightly downhill and then bear left along Saxon Road, which leads right in about 200m to the entrance to Nuns Road. Take the waymarked **St Swithun's Way** along the tarmac footpath, which is slightly obscured just a few metres on the left.

2 Continue to a narrow roadway and cross directly to another path and Hillier's Haven, part of the adjoining woodland on the right. Keep to the broadening path before edging left and passing the pedestrian entrance to Chalkpit Cottage Farm a few metres further on. Continue alongside the **Winnall Moors nature reserve**. This 64-hectare Site of Special Scientific Interest is noted for its rich wild-flower population.

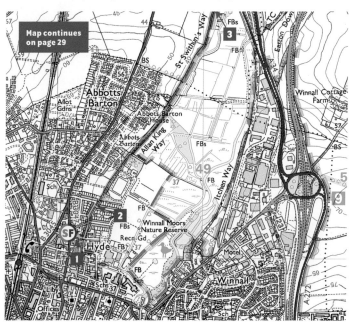

Map continues on page 29

Winnall Moors nature reserve

3 Towards the end of the reserve is an information board quite close to the path. In another 200m you pass a large black pipe straddling a narrow stream. The A34 dual carriageway is just above you. Keep to its base before negotiating subways under the two sections of the road. At the end of the second subway the footpath continues around to the left. A kissing gate in a few metres opens onto a tarmac path bisecting a site occupied by modern office buildings. Go through the car park to another kissing gate and past a short row of houses to St Mary's churchyard in **Kings Worthy**.

> ⓘ *The underlying chalk of much of southern England, including Winchester, was formed during the Upper Cretaceous geological period 99–66 million years ago.*

Thatched cottages at Easton

4 At the corner of the church tower and entrance door bear sharp right and through the churchyard to a fingerpost by the entrance to St Mary's Close. The Old Post Office, now a private residence, is on the left. Continue along St Mary's Close and through the garage area for about 100m to the **A33**. Cross the road at the two-part pedestrian crossing. On the other side of the road carefully go down the bank to a woodland path that in about 350m takes you to the bottom of Mill Lane in **Abbots Worthy**. Turn right along Mill Lane, following the Itchen Way through some open scrubland to a metal kissing gate and across several channels of the

River Itchen for about 450m, to reach Fulling Mill Cottage and its extensive grounds. To shorten your walk you can retrace your route from here to Hyde Gate.

5 Cross the frontage of Fulling Mill Cottage and exit from the far side. The Itchen Way now diverts as the fingerpost ahead confirms, but ignore that and instead turn directly left through the parking area to a narrow corridor of tall trees leading to a fenced and broader path alongside the base of the **M3** to a subway. On the other side of the subway the fenced path continues for about 125m to a path junction.

6 Turn left through more scrubland for a short distance to reach a gap in the hedge, which opens out into a large rising field. Keep to the left-hand boundary, heading towards the stile in the far left-hand corner of the field. As you clamber across the stile you can see the Church of St Mary a few hundred metres away in **Easton**. As you approach the church the path moves to the right and through a kissing gate, shortly after which you join a narrow access road that continues left to the main part of the village.

7 After exploring Easton, with its many thatched buildings, simply retrace your outward route to Hyde Gate.

– To shorten

Walk as far as Fulling Mill Cottage and retrace your route to the start, saving about 45min.

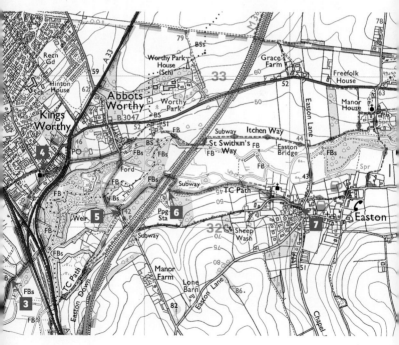

South Downs Way on the edge of Winchester

WALK 4

Chilcomb and the South Downs Way

Time: 2hr
Distance: 8km (5 miles)
Climb: 75m

Straightforward walk along part of the South Downs Way to the chalk downland village of Chilcomb in the South Downs National Park

Start/finish	*King Alfred's statue in the Broadway*
Locate	*SO23 9BE ///paraded.margin.bulge*
Cafes/pubs	*Lots of pubs and cafes in Winchester*
Transport	*Train to Winchester*
Parking	*Park and Ride outside the city and plenty of parking in the centre*
Toilets	*In Abbey Gardens by the Broadway*

This out-and-back walk takes you for part of the first stage of the South Downs Way from Winchester to the downland village of Chilcomb with its Grade 1 listed 12th-century flint church. Initially you follow the River Itchen towards Wolvesey Castle then head through the eastern part of the city and on to Chilcomb along the top edge of a sweeping downland field with far-reaching views.

Looking towards Winchester from Chilcomb

1 From the back of King Alfred walk about 100m towards the road bridge over the cascading River Itchen. At the bridge follow the sign for the South Downs Way (SDW) and Viaduct Way as you descend a ramp and short flight of steps to the broad tarmac path called The Weirs. Keep to the path for about 500m as it draws alongside the medieval flint wall edging around to the right and marking the boundary with the remnants of **Wolvesey Castle** (see Walk 5). As you reach the entrance to Wolvesey bear left along College Walk which continues as the combined route of the SDW and Viaduct Way.

> ⓘ *It has been suggested that the Cornish granite plinth supporting King Alfred's statue may be the wrong way up!*

2 Continue along College Walk for about 100m to the junction with a college access road. Turn left for about 200m, still along College Walk, to reach the residential road Wharf Hill, where the SDW departs to the left. Follow Wharf Hill for about 200m uphill to reach a set of crossroads at the bottom of East Hill.

3 Head up East Hill as the SDW direction post indicates. A little further on the SDW forks along Petersfield Road

King Alfred

ÆLFRED

to the right. After about another 450m the road divides at Fivefields Road but you keep straight ahead towards a 'No through road' sign. Ignore the turning on the left to Chalk Ridge and continue along the tarmac path through a short avenue of trees fronted by a set of posts. At the end of the avenue follow the SDW fingerpost pointing right – still slightly uphill – along the tarmac path. At the top of the path cross a pedestrian bridge above the **M3**. At the end of the bridge go left for a few metres to a gap through the hedge. Across the valley is Ministry of Defence land and you should just be able to make out the Chilcomb firing range.

4 Continue along the SDW for another 1km to reach the village of **Chilcomb**. Go through a gap in the hedgerow and down a short flight of improvised steps onto narrow **Chilcomb Lane** and follow the signpost on the other side pointing left to St Andrew's Church. Keep along the SDW around to the right for 200m to a fork in the road. Take the right-hand fork, leaving the SDW, and continue for about 500m to the church.

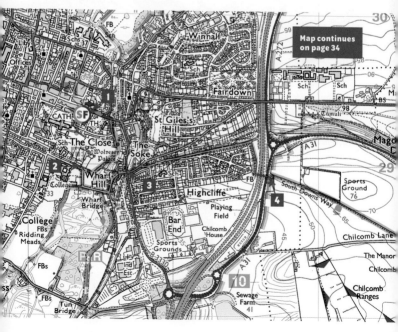

Map continues on page 34

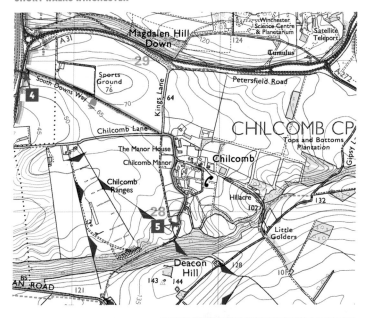

The Church of St Andrew is early 12th-century Norman, largely flint built, and Grade 1 listed. It is little altered from when it was originally constructed in the time of William the Conqueror.

5 Following your visit to St Andrew's Church it's a straightforward return to Alfred in the Broadway.

St Andrew's Church, Chilcomb

WALK 5
City Mill, St Giles Hill and Wolvesey Castle

Start/finish	*King Alfred's statue in the Broadway*
Locate	*SO23 9BE ///paraded.margin.bulge*
Cafes/pubs	*Lots of pubs and cafes in Winchester*
Transport	*Train to Winchester*
Parking	*Park and Ride outside the city and plenty of parking in the centre*
Toilets	*In Abbey Gardens by the Broadway*

It's a relatively steep climb up to the viewing platform on St Giles Hill, but your reward is a panoramic view of Winchester. The descent is back to the River Itchen and the medieval ruins of Wolvesey Castle.

Time: 1hr
Distance: 3km (1¾ miles)
Climb: 50m

A panoramic view of Winchester and the medieval seat of power of the Norman bishops, Wolvesey Castle

View from Blue Ball Hill

1 From the back of King Alfred make your way about 100m towards the road bridge over the River Itchen and cross the road to the City Mill. The City Mill has been restored by the National Trust to full working order and now produces flour for sale.

City Mill

2 Facing the City Mill bear right along the pavement, ignoring Water Lane on the left as you continue to St John's Street a few metres further on. Turn left into this narrow street which is quite uphill. Pass the flint-built **Church of St John the Baptist** to arrive at a resplendent white house, a former inn, now known as The Old Blue Boar.

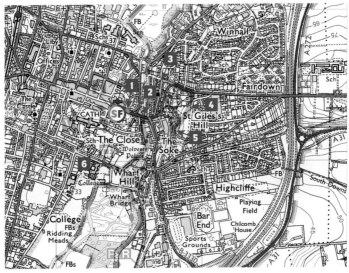

The Old Blue Boar, a former inn

The Old Blue Boar is a traditional hall house with a projecting gallery. It was built around 1340, about eight years before the Black Death, and is said to be the oldest civil building in Winchester.

3 Bear right at the junction with Blue Ball Hill and continue uphill to the main road, Magdalen Hill. Cross the road and ignore the first tarmac access path to the right with a street sign 'St Giles Hill private road'. Continue instead along the raised path with a handrail barrier parallel to the main road for about another 70m to a second tarmac path, also displaying a St Giles Hill street sign. Here turn right and at the top emerge onto an undulating green known as **St Giles Hill**, surrounded by mature trees. In medieval times large markets were held on this site, attended by merchants from various parts of the globe. Continue the few metres to the crest of grass just in front of you.

4 Cross to the obscured viewing platform about 150m away, keeping to the left of a lamppost and aiming for a point roughly halfway along the line of trees at the lower edge of the green. You will now be able to see most of Winchester, including Alfred's statue.

View over Winchester from St Giles Hill

5 Now retrace your outward route past The Old Blue Boar to the City Mill (Waypoint 2). With your back to the City Mill cross to the other side of the bridge and turn left down the ramp and short flight of steps to the broad tarmac path called The Weirs by the side of the river. Keep to the path for about 500m as it draws alongside the medieval flint wall edging around to the right to reach the entrance to **Wolvesey Castle**. From here you can if you wish lengthen your walk towards St Cross (Walk 1).

6 Return to the bridge and turn left to King Alfred's statue.

+ To lengthen

At the entrance to Wolvesey Castle (Waypoint 6) continue along College Walk for about 100m then turn right along the college access road and join the waymarked Clarendon Way to the Hospital of St Cross. Return to Wolvesey and retrace your route back to King Alfred's statue, adding about another 3km and 1hr.

Wolvesey Castle

Remnants of medieval Wolvesey Castle

Wolvesey Castle was one of the most important buildings in medieval England. Although it is called a castle, originally it was more of a palace. Throughout the medieval period the bishops of Winchester arguably held one of the highest positions of power in the English church and in national politics. Wolvesey Castle, also known as the Old Bishop's Palace, was largely the creation of Bishop Henry of Blois, who was bishop for 42 years from 1129 until his death in 1171. On his arrival the building consisted only of one large hall. Henry added new buildings, including a keep, a defensive tower and two gatehouses. For opening times see www.english-heritage.org.uk.

Westgate

WALK 6
Westgate, St Cross and Shawford

Time: 1¾hr
Distance: 6.5km (4 miles)
Climb: 40m

A linear walk taking in the medieval Westgate, Winchester Cathedral and a 12th-century almshouse

Start	Westgate by the Great Hall
Finish	Shawford
Locate	SO23 9AP ///fond.letter.outpost
Cafes/pubs	Pubs and cafes in Winchester and Shawford
Transport	Regular train or bus service from Shawford back to Winchester
Parking	Park and Ride outside the city and plenty of parking in the centre
Toilets	Jewry St by Theatre Royal (300m off route)

This walk starts at Winchester's Westgate, near the Great Hall. After passing the Cathedral the route follows the Clarendon Way to St Cross and then joins the Itchen Way running for the most part alongside the Itchen Navigation southwards through the broad river valley, to end at Shawford.

Crossing the River Itchen with Hockley Viaduct in the distance

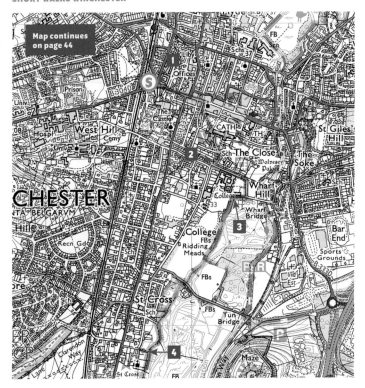

Map continues on page 44

The Westgate (now incorporating a museum) is a medieval replacement. The original gate was built by the Romans, who occupied the city for more than three centuries. The nearby Great Hall is one of the finest surviving aisled halls of the 13th century and displays a replica of mythological King Arthur's Round Table.

1 From the Westgate follow the High Street, dropping gently down towards the city centre. Within about 150m cross Southgate Street and continue towards the overhanging clock and on to the Butter Cross. The Butter Cross dates from the 15th century and was restored in 1865. As its name suggests, it was sometimes used for the sale of produce. Now bear to the right below an archway leading to the avenue of trees that brings you to the front of the majestic Cathedral, consecrated in 1093. Go towards the Cathedral's right-hand corner and through the stone archway into The Close. At the end of The Close is the 15th-century Priors Gate, which leads to the 14th-century Kingsgate with the 'miniature' Church of St Swithun-upon-Kingsgate above.

2 Leave under the Kingsgate and turn left into College Street. On your right you pass the house where the writer Jane Austen spent the last months of her life in 1817. Continue to the end of College Street and bear right at the road barrier into College Walk, keeping alongside the brick wall for about 100m to a junction. Turn right along the college access road to where it shortly ends by a fingerpost with a Clarendon Way waymark disc pointing left.

> ⓘ *The Great Hall is all that survives of Winchester Castle, most of which was destroyed on the orders of Oliver Cromwell.*

3 Turn left and continue for about 650m to Garnier Road where you cross to a second Clarendon Way fingerpost slightly to the right. Another 500m with views opening out brings you to the **Hospital of St Cross** and Almshouse of Noble Poverty (see Walk 1).

4 The Clarendon Way diverts to the right at St Cross, but you instead keep straight along the path to a metal kissing gate at the beginning of a short avenue of trees followed by another kissing gate at the end, a third further on and finally a single gate that in a few metres leads to a narrow tarmac closed road, Five Bridges Road. Turn left and continue to the road end. As you cross the River Itchen you will see on your right the former railway viaduct in the distance at Hockley.

The house where novelist Jane Austen died

5 Go through the gate to a junction of tarmac paths where the **Itchen Way** (IW) now joins. Take the path signposted Itchen Navigation Southampton, which quickly leads down to an M3 single slip road and a pedestrian crossing. Cross the road to the pavement on the other side. Do not immediately follow the IW under the bridge but instead go about 50m to the right and take a footpath that shortly leads under another part of the M3. Soon the IW re-joins from the left. Continue alongside the Itchen Navigation and through the flat and open river valley. Keep to the IW towards Shawford, passing the remnant of **Compton Lock**, once part of the Itchen Navigation.

Remnant of Compton Lock

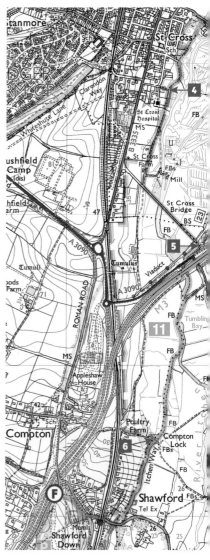

Shawford Down

6 Follow the IW to join the road through **Shawford** and turn right towards Shawford station. If you intend to catch the bus back to Winchester, continue beyond the station for a few metres to the car park at the bottom of **Shawford Down** where there are a couple of entrance gates. Go through the right-hand gate and follow the path alongside the boundary of the Down uphill for about 200m until you can see across to the left a metal kissing gate fronting a gap in the hedge at the top. This leads out to the bus stop on the other side of the road.

+ To lengthen

At Waypoint 5 turn sharp right, signposted for the Viaduct Way (National Cycle Route 23), to visit the Hockley railway viaduct, adding about 500m each way and 20min. Return to Waypoint 5 to continue the walk.

Near the start of the walk at Cheriton

WALK 7

Cheriton, Hinton Ampner and Kilmeston

Time: 2hr
Distance: 7.5km (4¾ miles)
Climb: 135m

An English Civil War battle site and delightful parkland at Hinton Ampner in the South Downs National Park

Start/finish	School Road, Cheriton (opposite primary school)
Locate	SO24 0QA ///author.gaps.contained
Cafes/pubs	Pubs in Cheriton and Hinton Ampner (650m off route)
Transport	Bus from Winchester
Parking	Roadside parking in Cheriton
Toilets	No public toilets on route

Apart from the optional section to visit Cheriton Wood, this out-and-back walk follows the Wayfarer's Walk to the National Trust's Hinton Ampner country house and the glorious South Downs parkland taking you to the downland village of Kilmeston. Return is by the same route.

South Downs at Hinton Ampner

1 Start from the road on the other side of the stream in front of the primary school. Cross the small bridge and follow the short residential access road to the right. On the wall of the bridge an old metal notice warns that the bridge is only strong enough to 'carry ordinary traffic'. At the end of the access road the Wayfarer's Walk (WW) is signed to the left up a narrow enclosed path. The Itchen Way is also waymarked as it follows the same route at the beginning. The path opens out as you reach the top of the incline, with elevated **Cheriton Wood** on the skyline in the distance.

Wayfarer's Walk at Cheriton

2 Continue along the fenced path around the field boundary towards the far right-hand corner where the Itchen Way departs along a broad grassy track to the right. Stay with the WW instead, which continues straight on for about 450m to another broad grassy track crossover. At this point you can if you wish lengthen the walk immediately ahead to visit historic Cheriton Wood.

3 From the crossover follow the broad grassy track to the right, designated a restricted byway, going gradually downhill towards Hinton Ampner, and in about 300m you will cross another broad grassy track. Continue for about a further 350m to a very modest information board on the right describing the Battle of Cheriton.

Cheriton Wood was probably where the English Civil War battle on the 29th March 1644 began. It was closely fought but ended in victory for the Parliamentarians and is likely to have paved the way for the eventual defeat and execution of Charles 1.

4 Now cross the busy A272 just a short distance ahead and continue up the narrow lane on the other side through **Hinton Ampner** to a set of full-size wrought-iron gates. If the gates are closed there is a gap on the

Cheriton Wood, part of the Civil War battle site

left to pass through. In just a few more metres and opposite the 13th-century Church of All Saints go through the first gate on the left, ignoring the second gate behind it.

> (i) *Winchester was at the centre of sustained and extensive conflict during the English Civil War in the 1640s.*

5 Turn immediately right and follow the footpath (which can be muddy at times) downhill alongside the boundary hedge with Hinton Ampner House to a gate that opens onto a broad track. The source of the River Itchen is a few hundred metres to the right. Go through a kissing gate on the other side of the track and into the gloriously expansive South Downs parkland. Continue slightly uphill to a second kissing gate by some trees, and from this vantage point you will be able to see **Hinton Ampner House** emerging grandly into view behind you. Ahead is another kissing gate, following which the WW begins to edge towards a wall on the right.

6 You will soon reach a stile onto a narrow lane at **Kilmeston** and the Church of St Andrew 50m to the right, which marks the end of this first part of your journey. The second part is to retrace your route to Cheriton. If you did not pay a visit to Cheriton Wood on the way out you have that option on your way back!

Looking across to Hinton Ampner House from the Wayfarer's Walk

━ To shorten

Stop at Hinton Ampner and retrace your route to Cheriton, saving about 2.5km and 40min.

✚ To lengthen

For a pleasant and historic diversion, at the track crossover at Waypoint 3 continue straight ahead through a gap in the hedge for about 750m each way to the corner of Cheriton Wood, adding about 25min.

Hinton Ampner House

The original building at Hinton Ampner was a Tudor manor house built in about 1540, most of which was demolished in 1793 and subsequently replaced. The only part of the original building that remains is the stable, now used as a cafe. Ralph Dutton inherited the estate in 1935 and gradually converted the property into the Neo-Georgian country house it is today. Following his death in 1985 the estate was bequeathed to the National Trust. For opening times see www.nationaltrust.org.uk.

Top: former fulling mill astride the River Alre. Left: Broad Street, New Alresford.
Right: restricted byway from Abbotstone to Old Alresford

WALK 8

New Alresford, Abbotstone and Old Alresford

Start/finish	*Broad Street, New Alresford*
Locate	*SO24 9AQ ///kindness.renewals.defining*
Cafes/pubs	*Pubs and cafes in New Alresford*
Transport	*Bus from Winchester*
Parking	*New Alresford*
Toilets	*By the heritage railway station car park (about 250m off route)*

Time: 2½hr
Distance: 9km (5½ miles)
Climb: 110m

A circular walk following chalk streams and visiting the exquisite Georgian town of New Alresford

This circuit of infinite variety includes a charming 13th-century fulling mill, a restored eel house, the medieval Three Castles Path and a poignant RAF commemorative platform overlooking Abbotstone. It begins and ends in the lovely town of New Alresford, with its Watercress Line heritage steam railway.

Watercress Line heritage railway station

New Alresford is an outstanding Georgian market town. Much of it was rebuilt in the 18th century after a devastating fire in 1689 and another in 1736. Rising phoenix-like from the ashes, the town has developed a very distinctive look and feel and has retained its original street pattern.

1 Start in Broad Street and head down to Mill Hill and then Ladywell Lane, which goes sharply to the left towards the chalk stream **River Alre**, a tributary of the River Itchen. The Wayfarer's Walk (WW) follows alongside the Alre, passing the splendid 13th-century former fulling mill to reach a road end. A fulling mill used water-powered wooden hammers to shrink and tighten raw and unfinished cloth, making it more closely woven.

2 The Alre and the WW divert sharply in the signposted direction of the eel house, which you reach after several hundred metres. Cross the narrow footbridge around the eel house and continue along an enclosed path to a gate that opens onto a small fenced and hedged section of grass and a few trees. Cross to the well-fenced path straight ahead that rises slightly uphill to meet a narrow lane.

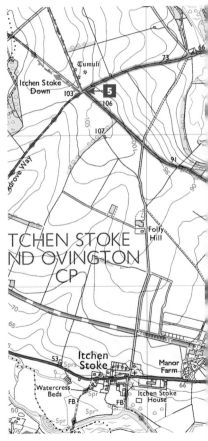

(i) *A crop heavily reliant on chalk streams is watercress, which thrives in the clean, mineral-rich and well-oxygenated water.*

The eel house dates from the 1820s. It last provided eels on a commercial basis around 1980 but gradually fell into disrepair. In 2006 a major restoration project was undertaken, and the eel house has been restored to basic working order, although it is no longer commercially operational.

3 Continue left along the lane for about 100m to where it curves around to the left. Leave the lane at this point and go under the height restriction

barrier on your right. Now keep to the woodland track for about 900m to another height restriction barrier marking a track junction.

4 Bear left under the barrier, which is also WW waymarked, to be greeted by the sound of a rushing stream (unseen). Continue along the woodland track, passing a flint-built house on the right, to reach a height restriction barrier, by a narrow lane. A commemorative information board here records the tragic loss of three RAF pilots in 1944 during a simulated battle training exercise. Across the lane is yet another height restriction barrier fronting an enclosed restricted byway that leads in about 500m to a track junction and an unusual waymark fingerpost indicating the route of the Three Castles Path.

This 60-mile route between Winchester and Windsor was inspired by the 13th-century journeys of King John. Halfway along is the castle he built near Odiham in Hampshire.

5 Join the Three Castles Path going downhill to the right leading to the hamlet of **Abbotstone**. Continue past a short terrace of cottages to where the WW goes off to the left in the direction of Abbotstone Farm House and Abbotstone Barn. Ignore this and

Signs for Three Castles Path near Abbotstone

instead keep straight ahead for about 250m to a fingerpost marking another restricted byway.

6 Follow this broad track, which in about 2km brings you to the edge of the small village of **Old Alresford** and deposits you onto a narrow access lane. Follow the lane as it bears left past the playing field to the village hall where you turn right, crossing the main road to a tarmac footpath. Continue to the right for about 400m to a road junction with the Church of St Mary in front of you.

7 Re-cross the main road and continue along the footpath on the other side slightly downhill for about another 350m to a triangular road junction. Here you cross directly to a signposted and fenced footpath that takes you back to Mill Hill and the bottom of Broad Street in **New Alresford**.

WALK 9
Itchen Stoke and Ovington

Start/finish	Itchen Stoke village green
Locate	SO24 0QZ ///slogans.swimmer.aviators
Cafes/pubs	Pub in Ovington
Transport	Bus from Winchester
Parking	Small informal car park about 75m along a rough tarmac track by the side of the village green
Toilets	No public toilets on route

This is a gentle walk over chalk downland, starting alongside the River Itchen and continuing across open farmland, through woodland and along quiet lanes within the South Downs National Park. The route starts with the Itchen Way and explores the area around the delightful village of Ovington where it joins the St Swithun's Way before making a serene return over chalk downland back to Itchen Stoke.

Time: 1¾hr
Distance: 6.5km (4 miles)
Climb: 75m

A close encounter with the famous chalk stream the River Itchen and a village of classic flint and thatch

Bush Inn at Ovington

1 Cross the main road from the village green to visit redundant St Mary's Church. This colourful Victorian church was inspired by the 13th-century Sainte Chapelle in Paris, chapel of French kings. Re-cross and head past the car park along the rough tarmac track to a small bridge over a channel of the River Itchen, displaying an Itchen Way (IW) waymark. Once across the bridge keep alongside the river to the Bush Inn at **Ovington** where you join the St Swithun's Way linking Winchester Cathedral and Farnham in Surrey. Continue for about 150m slightly uphill to a large flint building on the corner of the junction with narrow **Lovington Lane**. Turn right, keeping to the lane for about 1km to Yavington Barn and the next-door Yavington Studio.

2 Within another 250m you will see a grey metal kissing gate on the left, waymarked St Swithun's Way plus the IW and some other waymarks. Go through the gate to a steep path that climbs back up for 50m towards another grey metal kissing gate close to a small group of trees and which opens out into a field. Go through the gate and immediately head left, keeping to the rising footpath alongside the boundary of the field towards its top edge, and in another few metres come to a short line of trees astride the ridge, with views over the downland valley.

River Itchen near Ovington

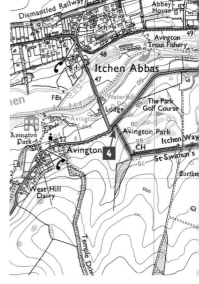

Between Ovington and Avington

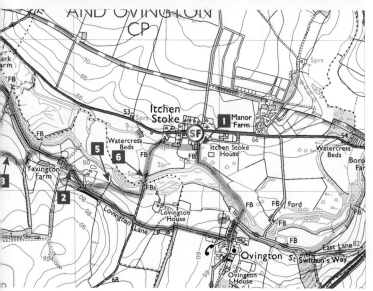

3 Continue for about 800m, skirting farmland to arrive at the car park for **Avington golf course**. Go past the golf course entrance and clubhouse and continue about 200m down the access track to reach a junction with a narrow lane, where you turn right. Over to the left you can see the elegant entrance gates of the Avington Park private estate.

4 Follow the lane for about 2km back to Yavington Barn. Opposite the entrance to Yavington Barn are a kissing gate and a fingerpost with a waymark for the IW. A sign on the gate says 'Please keep dogs on leads'. Go through the gate into a small field and stay on the path slightly uphill alongside the high hedge towards the right-hand corner and through two more kissing gates. Each has the same 'dogs on leads' directive as well as an IW waymark.

5 Continue slightly downhill across the field to a green metal kissing gate. The broad grassy path continues to another green metal kissing gate that opens out onto a woodland path junction. The IW goes to the left along the path, which at certain times of the

Golf course at Avington

Itchen Way at Yavington

year can be quite boggy in places. In a few metres cross a footbridge and go through yet another green metal kissing gate onto a flat open area of scrubland that can also be very soft underfoot.

6 Now head towards the far right-hand boundary and as you get there move to the right through a gap in the hedge to the adjoining meadow. Continue through the meadow towards the field gate you can see ahead next to a stile with an IW waymark. Do not clamber over the stile but instead bear right and go directly back to the car park about 250m away. This permissive detour courtesy of the landowner avoids the busy main road, which is the official route of the IW but is not safe as it lacks a pavement.

Chalk streams

Chalk streams like the River Itchen are sustained by well-oxygenated water full of minerals and nutrients. This helps to create communities of aquatic plants, including water crowfoot and starwort mid-channel, and watercress and lesser water-parsnip along the river edges. By slowing the water flow in the summer, these plants help to provide food and protection for invertebrates and fish including brown trout and salmon. Chalk streams are very rare. They naturally occur in those areas where chalk is the main geological feature. Water drains through the porous chalk to collect in aquifers that in turn release water to feed the springs, creating rivers such as the Itchen.

The approach to Martyr Worthy

WALK 10

Itchen Abbas, Martyr Worthy, Easton and Avington

Start/finish	St John the Baptist, Itchen Abbas
Locate	SO21 1BJ ///snowstorm.books.streak
Cafes/pubs	Pubs in Itchen Abbas and Easton
Transport	Bus from Winchester
Parking	Along the road between Itchen Abbas and Avington
Toilets	No public toilets on route

Time: 1¾hr
Distance: 7km (4¼ miles)
Climb: 65m

Meadows, woodland, the sparkling River Itchen and stunning Avington Park

This circular walk explores a series of charming thatched villages. Following the Itchen Way, you begin in Itchen Abbas and wander through sloping meadows to the hamlet of Chilland, where the River Itchen is in full flow, before continuing to Martyr Worthy. After crossing the Itchen, you arrive in the village of Easton. Avington House, set in glorious parkland, dramatically presents itself as you make your way back to Itchen Abbas.

Lychgate of St John the Baptist at Itchen Abbas

1 Pick up the combined Itchen Way (IW) and St Swithun's Way by the lychgate of the Church of St John the Baptist. Continue along the enclosed path to a gate that opens into a sloping meadow, with the **River Itchen** below. Stay along the top edge of the meadow overhung with mature trees for about 150m to a metal kissing gate and into more meadow. Follow the broad path to another kissing gate that opens onto a fenced and hedged footpath, leading you alongside a tall brick wall to a few improvised steps down to the narrow lane at **Chilland**.

2 Instead of continuing to the enclosed footpath the other side of the lane, first bear left for a short 100m detour past the former Chilland Mill to a footbridge over a particularly exuberant part of the Itchen. To shorten your walk continue along the footpath through a field for about another 350m to a road where you turn left back to Avington.

3 From the bridge retrace the 100m back to the enclosed footpath and rejoin the combined IW and St Swithun's Way that continue through meadow and a variety of IW-marked gates for about 800m to Martyr Worthy. As you get to **Martyr Worthy** continue along the short access way enclosed with shrubs and small trees leading to a narrow lane. Turn left onto the narrow

lane by St Swithun's Church, elements of which date back to the 12th century. At this point St Swithun's Way departs on its own back to Winchester.

4 Continue for about 100m to the left down the narrowing lane to reach a direction post with an IW waymark. In a few moments you will come to a footbridge and another very broad and lively section of the Itchen. Cross the bridge to a second smaller footbridge and then to a gate that leads out into a flat and open field. Follow the fence on your right to a distant corner post where you bear right towards a short access track leading to a gate

in a few metres around the corner. Go through the gate onto a stony access track, at the end of which is a narrow lane meandering between the charming villages of Easton and Avington.

The Old Post Office at Easton

5 Turn right along the lane and in about 100m you will come to a sharp left-hand bend followed by an IW way-marked fingerpost on the right about 50m further on. Keep to the IW as directed to emerge on the road the other side of **Easton**. Turn left and in about another 150m left again, continuing the circuit of the village that will bring you back to the IW fingerpost you followed at the start of the loop.

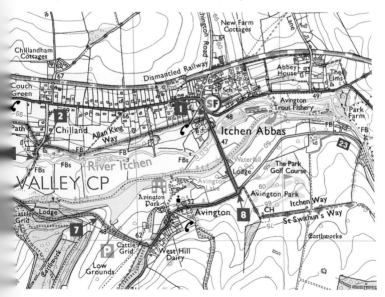

Looking across to Avington Park

6 Retrace your steps for about 150m to where you emerged from the stony access track earlier and instead, now leaving the IW, continue along the lane towards Avington. In about 600m the lane enters some woodland. As you leave the woodland after another 500m and bypass a cattle grid, breathtaking **Avington House** comes into view, set in classic parkland.

7 Continue slightly downhill, passing the lake in Avington Park, to a road junction where you turn left to **Avington**. Stay on the road through the village to a triangular junction and follow the road around to the left.

8 Continue towards Itchen Abbas, passing the elegant entrance gates and avenue of trees that lead to the front of Avington House. It is now just a few hundred metres back along the road to **Itchen Abbas**.

Itchen Abbas is where Charles Kingsley, a frequent visitor, was inspired to write his socially challenging classic novel *The Water Babies* in 1863. Kingsley was curate and then rector of Eversley in Hampshire. He also wrote *Westward Ho!* in 1855.

— To shorten

For a walk of about 4km that will take 1hr in total, leave the footbridge over the River Itchen at Chilland (Waypoint 3) and continue along the footpath for about 350m to the road between Easton and Avington. Turn left towards Avington and follow the road back to Itchen Abbas.

WALK 11
Stockbridge Down

Time: 1hr
Distance: 3.5km
(2¼ miles)
Climb: 75m

Stockbridge Down is chalk downland with spectacular views in most directions

Start/finish	*Stockbridge Down*
Locate	*SO20 6BY ///cooked.balance.fight*
Cafes/pubs	*None on route*
Transport	*No public transport*
Parking	*Car park at the eastern (Winchester) end of Stockbridge Down*
Toilets	*No public toilets on route*

The paths around Stockbridge Down make a labyrinthine patchwork which can be confusing at times, but on this walk you generally just keep to the external and sometimes ragged boundaries of the triangular-shaped Down. At about the halfway point, a spectacular view over the Test Valley opens up quite dramatically.

View northwards from Stockbridge Down

1 Go through the gate from the car park and immediately keep left along the slightly uphill path through light woodland to a wide and open area. Stay alongside the hedge and tree-lined boundary parallel with the road until you reach two single gates giving access from the larger National Trust car park on the other side of the **B3049**.

> ⓘ *Hampshire is synonymous with many writers, including Jane Austen, Thomas Hardy, Charles Dickens, Charles Kingsley, the naturalist Gilbert White and the 'compleat angler' Izaac Walton.*

2 When you are level with the gates bear half-right up the obvious path, moving away from the electricity poles in front of you. The track you now follow goes slightly uphill towards the end of the hedging and vegetation along the skyline. As you climb you will have glorious views of the wider Test Valley and the distant Danebury Hill Iron Age hill fort.

3 When you reach the fenced and tree-lined northern boundary of the Down bear right to join a rutted track rising gently before it soon moves away to the right. You instead keep straight on along the broad grassy path

dipping quickly downhill and then starting to rise before edging around to the left but still in line with the boundary. Keep to the boundary until you reach an earth bank and ditch, the remnants of part of **Woolbury Ring**.

> **Woolbury Ring is an Iron Age hill fort dating from about 2500 years ago and at 158m is the highest point on the Down. There are also 14 Bronze Age barrows or burial mounds protected as Scheduled Ancient Monuments.**

4 Stay parallel with the earth bank and ditch as you continue slightly uphill, avoiding the vegetation. At the top of a short rise the panoramic view begins to unfold. Ignore a couple of peripheral paths and keep more or

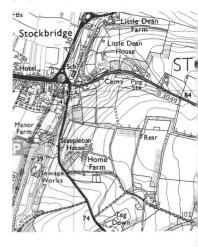

Remnants of Woolbury Ring

less straight ahead along the broad path as it descends sharply for about 200m, curving around to the left and towards light woodland below. Continue through the woodland and along a broad path with open and rising scrubland to your right.

Keep to the tree-lined boundary as the broad path continues for about another 300m, gradually descending to a path crossover. Go straight across and continue for about 350m to more light woodland and the gate that leads back into the car park.

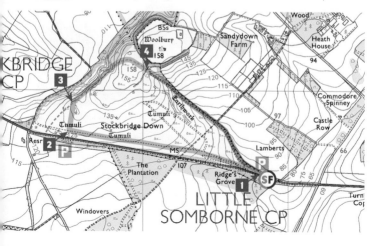

Free to roam on Stockbridge Down

Stockbridge Down

Stockbridge Down is a 65-hec-
tare area of grass chalk downland and was donated to the
National Trust in 1947. The
Down is managed principally
by grazing cattle, sheep and
horses, which helps maintain
the characteristics of the open
site. It is populated by an array
of wildlife, plants and wildflowers, including milkwort (which

Chalk hill blue butterfly

comes in a variety of colours, creating colourful patches), horseshoe vetch
and juniper. Slow-worms (one of six native reptile species in the UK) are
also found on the Down, as are a wide variety of butterflies, including in
summer the iconic chalk hill blue.

WALK 12
Stockbridge and Houghton

Start/finish	*Stockbridge High Street*
Locate	*SO20 6HF ///written.gashes.precluded*
Cafes/pubs	*Lots of pubs and cafes in Stockbridge*
Transport	*Infrequent bus service from Winchester*
Parking	*On-street parking in Stockbridge*
Toilets	*Stockbridge High Street*

From the High Street in Stockbridge this out-and-back walk takes you across the Common Marsh, a Site of Special Scientific Interest owned by the National Trust. You then join the Test Way along the former 'Sprat and Winkle' railway, which ran between Andover and Southampton until its closure in the 1960s. At the crossover with the Clarendon Way and Monarch's Way you turn right towards the footbridge over the timeless River Test at Houghton. The return is along the same route.

Time: 2¼hr
Distance: 9.5km (6 miles)
Climb: 25m

A level walk that follows the dismantled 'Sprat and Winkle' railway along the Test Way and the very finest of chalk streams, the River Test

Footbridge across the River Test at Houghton

Marshcourt River alongside the Common Marsh

1 On the southern side of Stockbridge High Street take the public footpath marked by a black fingerpost next to the former Lillie tearoom. The Lillie tearoom was named after Lillie Langtry who accompanied Edward Prince of Wales when he attended Stockbridge racecourse in the early 1870s. Follow the path through a double metal gate and by a narrow stream. Continue for about 400m until you reach the entrance to the **Common Marsh**.

2 Initially stay alongside the **Marshcourt River**. Further on and still keeping parallel to the river (although now at more of a distance) you will see over to the left the unmistakable Marsh Court. Continue in the general direction of the river to reach the tree-lined southern boundary of the common and then head towards the far left-hand corner. A boardwalk in front of the gate opens onto the Test Way, created from the track bed of the dismantled 'Sprat and Winkle' railway. The Test Way is a 71km (44 mile) long-distance trail from Inkpen Beacon in the North Wessex Downs to the Eling Tide Mill close to Southampton Water.

3 Turn right and continue along the Test Way for about 2km, passing **Yew Hill** just before the track crossover where the Test Way meets the combined Clarendon Way (the 38km-long former route used by pilgrims between Salisbury and Winchester) and the Monarch's Way.

Old St Peter's 12th-century church at Stockbridge

The 990km (615 miles) Monarch's Way follows the circuitous route taken by the 21-year-old Charles II in his flight from the Parliamentarians after his defeat at the Battle of Worcester in 1651. It ends at Shoreham-by-Sea in West Sussex.

4 Here you turn right towards Houghton, about 1km away. Cross several channels of the River Test before coming to the footbridge at **Houghton**, which presides over the expansive river in broad and majestic flow.

5 Retrace the 1km to the track cross-over and turn left to re-join the Test Way until you reach the gate where you left the common at Waypoint 3.

6 Do not go back through the gate, but continue along the Test Way for about 1.5km to the roundabout at the eastern entrance to **Stockbridge** and then turn left into the High Street. If you prefer, you can retrace your outward route back across the common into Stockbridge – the overall distance is about the same.

Marsh Court

This grandiose property was designed by Sir Edwin Lutyens and is a classic example of an English country house of the early Edwardian period. It was built between 1901 and 1904, although the ballroom, also designed by Lutyens, was added later in 1926. Using chalk as a building material, Marsh Court has a unique construction and a fairly colourful history to match. During World War 1 it was converted to a 60-bed military hospital. Marsh Court has also been used as a school.

Marsh Court

Church of St Mary at Micheldever

WALK 13

Micheldever, Stoke Charity, Hunton and Wonston

Start/finish	Duke Street, Micheldever
Locate	SO21 3DF ///plod.doctors.drummers
Cafes/pubs	Pubs in Micheldever and Wonston
Transport	No public transport
Parking	Playing field car park
Toilets	No public toilets on route

Time: 2¾hr
Distance: 10.5km (6½ miles)
Climb: 85m

A gentle walk exploring captivating flint-built villages and hamlets by the lovely River Dever

A gently undulating circuit, mainly along quiet country lanes and at times close to the chalk stream, the River Dever. It starts in the largely thatched village of Micheldever and continues to the charming hamlet of Weston Colley and past the quaintly named Stoke Charity, followed by glorious riverside Hunton and finally a circuit of another downland village, Wonston. Its Church of the Holy Trinity is one of the earliest documented churches in Hampshire, dating from AD901.

Between Weston Colley and Stoke Charity

River Dever at Stoke Charity

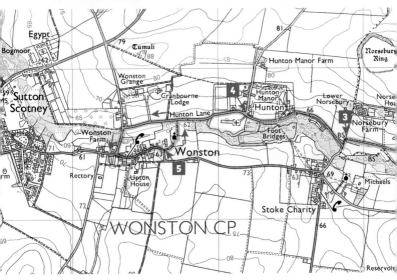

1 Leave the car park and cross the small bridge to a children's play area. Continue along the footpath by the side of a field beyond the play area, edging around to the left and into Rook Lane. At the end of Rook Lane turn right and continue along Church Street, crossing the nascent River Dever to a road junction signposted left for Weston Colley. Follow the narrow road slightly uphill as it goes under a mainline railway bridge before descending into the hamlet of **Weston Colley**.

2 Bear left and continue for about 450m to a sharp left-hand bend. Here leave the road and follow the tarmac access track to the five-barred gate

you can see ahead. Go through the pedestrian gate on the left-hand side and keep along the track for about 550m to where it bends to the right. Leave the track now and continue straight ahead across a short grassy section to an enclosed path for about 250m to reach a stile fronting a very narrow lane at **Stoke Charity**.

3 On the other side of the stile bear left for a few metres to join Hunton Lane, where you turn right towards the hamlet of **Hunton**. Continue along Hunton Lane for about 750m to a road junction with Hunton Down Lane and a small cluster of thatched cottages.

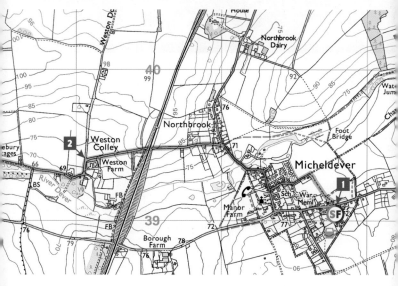

Spring in the Dever valley

4 Continue along Hunton Lane for 850m to another road junction, and then turn left for the 150m to **Wonston** and left again along the road sign-posted Micheldever. In about 350m you will reach the tarmac approach to Holy Trinity Church.

5 Go through the lychgate and in just a few metres turn right along the path between the gravestones towards a kissing gate bearing a footpath way-mark. Continue across the meadow to a footbridge and a second shorter footbridge leading to another kissing gate (which you passed earlier) open-ing onto Hunton Lane. Turn right, back towards Hunton. As you reach Hunton a fenced footpath at an angle on the right leads to the attractive St James' Church, which is worth a visit. Continue along Hunton Lane to where you joined it initially and bear left the few metres to the stile on the right you climbed over earlier. You can now retrace your outward route to Weston Colley and back to the playing field car park in Micheldever.

– To shorten

Stop at Hunton (leaving out the loop around Wonston), reducing the total distance by about 2km and saving about 30min.

The Swing Riots

In 1830 Micheldever was a flashpoint of labour unrest during the Swing Riots that were widespread throughout southern and eastern England. Farm labourers protested about their working conditions, and some resorted to destroying the new threshing machines that threatened their livelihood. One unfortunate protester from Micheldever, the young Henry Cook, was hanged at Winchester having been found guilty of an unfounded charge of attempted murder of a member of the local aristocracy. William Cobbett, a firebrand campaigner who was from Hampshire, supported the protesters. He also championed the repeal of the Corn Laws and the adoption of the Great Reform Act 1832.

Thatched cottages at Hunton

River Test at Chilbolton Cow Common

WALK 14

Wherwell and Chilbolton Cow Common

Start/finish	Wherwell sports field car park just past the primary school
Locate	SP11 7JP ///fancy.compelled.something
Cafes/pubs	Pubs in Wherwell and Chilbolton
Transport	No public transport
Parking	Car park at sports field
Toilets	No public toilets on route

Time: 1¼hr
Distance: 5km (3 miles)
Climb: 25m

This walk showcases pastoral England at its very best as you cross the River Test and wander through Chilbolton Cow Common

This circular walk starts near a channel of the River Test and continues slightly uphill through Wherwell to Chilbolton Cow Common. After completing a circuit of the common you return to Wherwell, passing the entrance to the site of the former Anglo-Saxon monastery Wherwell Abbey, destroyed in the 16th century.

Shepherds Cottage at Wherwell

The Longbridge across the River Test

1 Leave the car park and keep left along the **B3408** Longparish road, passing first the primary school and then thatched Shepherds Cottage at the junction with the B3420 Winchester Road. Continue straight ahead, slightly uphill for about 500m through the village of **Wherwell**. Wherwell is an especially attractive village of thatch and flint and played a prominent part in the Anglo-Saxon history of England. The gradient increases as you get to a sharp right-hand bend by the White Lion Inn.

2 At this point leave the B3420 and keep straight ahead (noting Mill Lane on your left for your return route) along the narrow Fullerton Road for about another 500m to reach the Longbridge on the left across the River Test.

> (i) *The water meadows irrigation system which operated during the 17th to 19th centuries was very effective before fertilizer became generally available.*

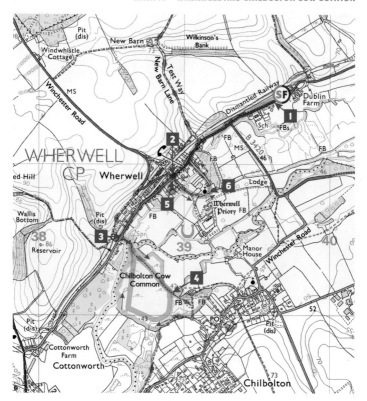

3 Cross the bridge, which is also part of the Test Way long-distance walking trail (see Walk 12). On the other side of the Longbridge is the entrance to Chilbolton Cow Common. Go into the common and continue straight ahead along the Test Way towards a smaller footbridge that crosses another channel of the river.

A remnant of a former water meadow with the River Test running alongside, Chilbolton Cow Common is designated a Site of Special Scientific Interest for its diverse ecosystem. It hosts many species of butterfly, wild plants, flowers and wetland birdlife, including heron, kingfisher and egret.

Snake's head fritillary on Chilbolton Cow Common

4 Just before you reach the foot-bridge bear right and follow the grassy track circumnavigating the common to arrive back at the Longbridge. Re-cross the bridge and retrace your route to Mill Lane.

5 Turn right at Mill Lane for about 150m to a triangular area of grass. Ahead is the access to the site of Wherwell Abbey, destroyed during Henry VIII's Dissolution of the Monasteries. Wherwell Priory, a large country house, now stands on the site. Bear left across the grass to the churchyard of St Peter and Holy Cross Church.

6 Go through the churchyard and exit under the lychgate into charming Church Street that halfway along crosses another delightful stretch of the River Test. Continue past the War Memorial and the thatched cottages on the corner and around to the right to re-join the road back to the car park, passing the main entrance to Wherwell Priory on the way.

River Test at Church St Wherwell

Queen Elfrida and Wherwell Abbey

Anglo-Saxon Queen Elfrida was married to King Edgar in AD964, becoming the first Queen of England. Elfrida founded the abbey in Wherwell in AD986. It is thought this was in atonement for the part she allegedly played in helping to orchestrate the assassination of King Edward the Martyr, Edgar's son from his first marriage. Elfrida's own son with Edgar – Ethelred the Unready – subsequently became king in place of his older half-brother Edward, a betrayal that led to unintended and unfortunate consequences, culminating in the Norman Conquest.

Heading away from Upper Mill

WALK 15
Longparish

Start/finish	Car park opposite Longparish village hall
Locate	SP11 6PB ///licks.smoker.owes
Cafes/pubs	Two pubs in Longparish
Transport	No public transport
Parking	Car park opposite village hall
Toilets	No public toilets on route

Time: 1½hr
Distance: 6km (3¾ miles)
Climb: 5m

A tranquil world of meadow paths and quiet lanes with the 'gin clear' water of the River Test nearby

A circuit of quiet lanes and meadow paths around the thatched linear village of Longparish. Shortly after the start the route passes the Church of St Nicholas, with its commemorative Aviator's Window, before continuing across several channels of the River Test to a fishery with a wide variety of wildlife. A partially restored former watermill and a wander through attractive parkland only add to the enjoyment.

Fishery at Longparish

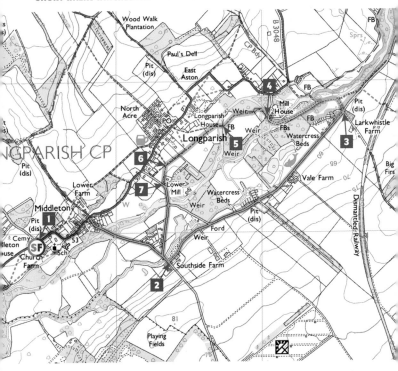

St Nicholas' Church dates from the 12th century, although the tower was constructed in the 16th century with stone taken from the dismantled Wherwell Abbey. In 1968 the Aviator's Window was installed in memory of Major Lanoe George Hawker VC, a World War 1 pilot killed in France in 1916.

1 From the car park opposite the village hall follow the pavement as it curves around to the right towards the primary school and the **Church of St Nicholas**. Keep to the pavement in front of the school playing field for about 200m to Southside Road where you turn right. To the left at the crossroads is Sugar Lane, which acquired its name when sugar beet was grown in the area. Continue along Southside Road for about 600m to pass Mill Lane on the left and cross a short road bridge over a tree-lined stream, part of the adjoining fishery.

> ⓘ *From May to August cutting to remove aquatic plants to improve the flow of chalk streams is carried out using a hand scythe.*

2 On the other side of the bridge turn left into Nuns Walk and continue for about 1.5km to a junction with a narrow access lane on the left. The rough track on the right serves **Larkwhistle Farm**.

3 Turn left and follow the lane to reach the River Test just ahead, which is usually fairly quiet and sedate here compared with elsewhere. After a short distance you will see a footpath and a footbridge to the right but ignore both and continue along the lane parallel with the river for about 350m to the partially restored **Upper Mill** (next to Mill House) and the sound of cascading water. Where the lane ends by the side of Upper Mill, keep straight ahead to the hedged footpath, as directed by the fingerpost.

4 The footpath soon leads to an old footbridge and then to a large

Upper Mill

Parkland at Longparish

meadow. Follow the well-fenced and hedged path alongside the meadow for about 300m to a more substantial footbridge across the river.

This area was once part of a water meadow natural irrigation system in use from the 17th to the 19th centuries. In the winter and early spring water would be redirected from the River Test to warm the grassland and add nutrients, thus promoting extra and earlier growth.

5 At the end of the bridge go through a kissing gate, which opens out to parkland with a dividing fence (including a stile) running across it. You now have a choice either to go directly towards the stile or to go through a second kissing gate just ahead and turn left alongside the fence to reach the stile. Either way, with your back now to the stile cross the parkland in front of you in a straight line for about 250m to a third kissing gate in the far right-hand corner at the end of a holly hedge. This gate leads out into more meadow with a variety of trees.

Autumn colour at Longparish

Replica stocks outside St Nicholas' Church at Longparish

6 Continue towards a fingerpost 50m away more or less straight ahead. As you reach it go towards the far left-hand corner of the meadow and exit through yet another kissing gate and a gap in the hedge fronting Mill Lane.

7 Bear left a few metres along Mill Lane and around the corner to a road bridge over a particularly lively section of the River Test, which is part of the fly-fishing beat at **Lower Mill**. Continue to the end of Mill Lane and the junction with Southside Road. Turn right and walk back to the car park.

USEFUL INFORMATION

Tourism organisations

The National Trust

www.nationaltrust.org.uk

English Heritage

www.english-heritage.org.uk

Visit Hampshire

www.visit-hampshire.co.uk

Accommodation

www.booking.com

www.trivago.co.uk

www.airbnb.co.uk

choosewhere.com

Tourist information centre

Winchester Guildhall, High Street

tel 01962 840500, www.visitwinchester.co.uk

Wildlife trust

Hampshire and Isle of Wight Wildlife Trust

www.hiwwt.org.uk